THE
RECRUITING
ACCELERATOR

ISBN 978-1-7343817-4-0 (paperback)

ISBN 978-1-7343817-5-7 (eBook)

THE RECRUITING ACCELERATOR

STRATEGIES TO **INCREASE** RECRUITING AND DUPLICATION IN YOUR NETWORK MARKETING BUSINESS

ROB SPERRY

TGON Publishing

Discover the strategies in network marketing to increase sales, leads, duplication and recruiting. It all begins with the right mindset!

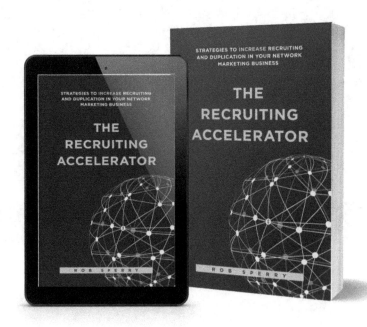

www.thegameofconquering.com

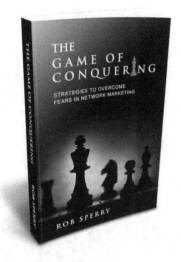

"You can make excuses or you can make money, but you can't do both."

I appreciate that you're driven and motivated to succeed in your networking marketing business (otherwise, why would you be reading this?), so I've gone all out for this Recruiting Accelerator eBook. I want you to experience the wild success I know you're capable of achieving, even if you don't realize it yet.

In this eBook, you'll get my Three-Tier System that will change the game for your business. I'll also reveal the **12 key strategies** from my 13 plus years as a network marketer that has allowed me to become the **number one recruiter out of a million distributors** and hit the top rank in a billion dollar company in just 10 months.

You'll get insight from high-level masterminds with six and seven-figure earners, information from top network marketing leaders and trainers, as well as a compact version of highlights from all my courses on network marketing. Are you ready for this? Let's do it!

BE THE RECRUITER FIRST

You know what you need to do to succeed in this business—become a great recruiter. This needs to be your **number one priority**, even if you're managing and training a team. The only way to successfully lead your team to earn 6 and 7 figures is by example.

I've seen it too many times where someone shifts their focus to getting their team to do the recruiting for them, for whatever reason. It could be fear, it could be laziness. If you find yourself slipping into management mode too often, take an honest look at your mindset and do the work to overcome any mental blocks you have around becoming a better recruiter. Become the dream team member that you would want to recruit, and stay out of management mode.

THE TEST BEFORE THE TESTIMONY

The next thing you must understand is that your success in this business is going to take time—a test that many people fail because they don't understand how it works.

Compensation always catches up to skill set and effort, but it's almost always **_massively_** _delayed_. Anyone you see giving their testimony on stage at conferences has first gone through the test of patience and persistence over time. Your journey is no different.

FOCUS: THE THREE-TIER SYSTEM

Billionaires don't work harder than millionaires. Many millionaires don't work harder than six-figure earners. Six-figure earners don't work harder than a lot of people who make minimum wage. It's *how* you spend your time that will be critical to your success.

Successful network marketers, the ones bringing in 5 and 6 figures per MONTH, are very disciplined and deliberate with their FOCUS. I based the Three-Tier System on the advice one of my mentors taught me about prioritizing my Income Generating Activities (or IPAs).

Think of this analogy. Tier One is the fire of your business. Tiers Two and Three are the fuel that grow your fire. However, if there's a ton of fuel and no fire to feed it to, you'll be running around being "busy" and getting zero results.

In order to be effective and have massive success, you MUST schedule in and spend **90% of your time on Tier One activities**. Once you do that, I promise you everything will change.

TIER ONE

1. Talk To Brand New People

This whole business revolves around talking to new people—schedule it in and plan it in detail, otherwise it will not get done. How many people are you going to reach out to? Who are you going to reach out to? What time are you going to reach out to those people? Out of all the Tier One steps, this is *the* most important one.

2. Third-Party Validation

You want your people to hear another perspective from someone else in the business to reinforce your credibility. This is called third-party validation. It could be including them in a group chat, a Zoom call or a three-way call with your upline. Live events are also great for third-party validation.

3. Add To Your Lead List

If the number one IPA is talking to new people, so you need to make sure your pipeline is always being filled. You must add to your lead list.

TIER TWO

1. Reach out to team members

If you're reaching out to your team members and encouraging them to do Tier One, they'll be doing third-party validations and putting you in front of new prospects. Guess what—you're accomplishing Tier One as well.

If they're not, you could get stuck focusing on being the super supportive "upline leader" and forgetting about Tier One for yourself. Whatever you do well *sometimes* duplicates within your team. Whatever you do poorly almost *always duplicates* within your team. You must become the leader you would want to recruit.

2. Nurture/Stay Connected With Your Leads

This doesn't mean fake chitchat. Find a mutual connection that you're genuinely interested in and have a real conversation with your leads.

The Greek Stoic philosopher Epictetus said, "We have two ears and one mouth so that we can listen twice as much as we speak." Always go into your conversations with a curious, giving mindset and really *listen*.

TIER THREE

1. Team trainings

Team trainings are very important to plug into as it gives you clarity on how to have success and can help feed your motivation.

2. Personal development

Many network marketing companies have personal development already worked into their systems. Tap into these after you've spent your time on Tier One activities. There are myriad podcasts and books on personal development that you can utilize.

One book that I really like is called "The Go-Giver" by Bob Burg and John D. Mann. It's a short and easy read, but will really help you understand the mindset you'll need to become a master recruiter.

3. Study anything relevant to your company

If you want to leverage your credibility, you should get to know the ins and outs of your company so that you can easily answer questions about it. Your company's history, backstory and product line/services are a great start. Once that's mastered, move onto other relevant info. Is there a specific technology around your company's product/services that you can delve deeper into? Get to know it all.

In my book **www.thegameofconquering.com** I go more in depth on The Income Producing Activities. I also give you my success formula. This formula has been used by all top earners but most haven't simplified the process it took them to have success.

THE 30 MILLION DOLLAR MENTOR

My 30 Million Dollar Mentor has been network marketing for 30 years. Before I was sponsored by him, I'd already known him for years. I had even taught his kids to play tennis. Once he convinced me to try the business, we had a conversation that has stuck in my mind to this day.

He asked me, "Rob, guess who the only person you're ever going to have to recruit is?"

I thought he meant what type of person, so I listed some. Maybe a person who's made millions, or a person who has great people skills.

My mentor said, "The only person you're ever going to have to recruit is yourself."

I said to him, "That's the stupidest thing I've ever heard. Are you kidding me? If I recruit myself and nobody else, I don't have a team. No one's going to order any product."

He said, "You don't get it."

I said, "What do you mean, I don't get it?"

Recruit Yourself

He said, "If you've truly recruited yourself, it's not a question of if, but when massive success happens for you. When you recruit yourself, you will believe in network marketing, in the products, the company, and in yourself. Everything else will fall into place. I can't promise you when, but I can promise you that it's going to happen for you."

This isn't to say you need to recruit yourself right away, especially if you're brand new to the business. You have your demons just like everyone else—mental barriers and limiting beliefs. It's important to be consciously aware of what you need to learn and then **take massive action on it.** You can't fully recruit yourself unless you stick to Tier One and actually talk to new people.

Find Your Battle Buddy

My mentor insisted that I needed a Battle Buddy, someone to go through the highs and the lows with. It could be a sideline, it could be your downline or it could be your upline.

Have Fun

Making money is fun. Helping other people make money is fun. Your dream job should be fun. Of course, there's lots of hard work involved and you're not going to love every single minute of it, but keep the attitude of fun and it will lift up those around you.

DAILY ACCOUNTABILITY

You might be super excited about the freedom of being your own boss, but **you will not achieve success without an accountability partner**. Find one, or make your battle buddy your accountability partner. This partner should be equally as committed to their business. Both of you need to set a daily accountability meeting and make sure you're sticking to Tier One activities.

A study referenced in **this article** shows that the probability that you will achieve your set goal is 95% when you have a specific accountability appointment with someone you've committed to.

Without these appointments, you're guaranteed to start spending too much time on Tiers Two and Three after hearing "no" too many times. You cannot let that stop you from forging ahead—don't let it stop your Battle Buddy, either. Be cheerleaders for each other, but show them tough love when you see that they need it.

DIRECT VS. INDIRECT APPROACH

In 2019, I did a study/survey of 138 committed network marketers from a variety of different companies about their relationship with their sponsor. The results are important for you to know because you need committed network marketers on your team, and you might be confused around the timing of your recruitment "ask".

- 15% said that they knew their sponsor for less than two months but more than a week.

- 41% knew their sponsor for less than a week.

- 44% knew their sponsor for more than a year.

The results are pretty evenly split between people who were recruited almost right away (less than a week), and people who knew their recruiter for a long time (more than a year).

What approach should you use, then?

Use the bold version of you to determine the best approach. There is no secret formula that you can just copy because we as humans are so complex, with different personalities and experiences. Depending on what works for you, direct is just as effective as indirect.

You can take the general principles of being direct or indirect and give them your own unique spin based on who you are and how you operate. This will take time to experiment with (remember, patience is key), but once you find your groove, that's when you'll start seeing results. This is the principle you'll be teaching to your team to duplicate your success.

12 KEY PRINCIPLES

People often confuse principles with techniques. You are unique, so you need to take these principles and make them work with your personality. The same goes for your team members; they aren't carbon copies of you, but they will be using the same principles to succeed.

Pick one of these principles and implement it regularly until it becomes second nature to you. Don't overwhelm yourself and think you need to do it all, because you may end up doing nothing.

1. Recruiting Mindset

When you recruit, you find what you're looking for. Your mindset must be focused on looking for customers and people who are interested in the business. Whatever you're looking for, your amazing subconscious mind will start building neuronal connections and find solutions for it.

2. Be Friends and Stay Friends

Let's say someone says no to your products or your business. That's fine. You can say something like, "Hey, can I keep you posted on my results?" or "Can I keep you posted on my success?" or "Can I reach out to you in the future?" Usually they'll say yes.

Once they say yes, what I do is put a couple of reminders in my phone to reach out once in a while. I comment on their posts or find something genuine to connect over, not fake chit chat. Maybe they just had a kid.

"Hey, congrats. I just saw you had your second kid!".

Maybe I just saw them post about a trip somewhere I want to travel to.

"Oh my goodness, that trip looked epic. I'd love to go there. What was your favorite part?"

3. Less Salesy, More Conversational

Listen to your prospects and ask good questions. Avoid being too directly salesy because that turns people off. You want to build a relationship first, and that requires conversation.

Questions Are The Answers by Allan Pease is a fantastic book to read to help you with this. Reading this book can go under Tier Three for personal development.

4. 90/10

When you're interacting with your leads, 90% of the conversation needs to be about them, only 10% about you. Remember, questions are the answers.

5. Posture

How would the million dollar version of you speak? How would you walk? What words would the best version of you use when you speak? You've got to become it in your mind for you to become it later.

6. Leverage Credibility

"But Rob, I don't have the credibility yet!" There's great power in leveraging your future credibility. Remember, most businesses don't turn a profit for three years. If you wait **three years** to feel credible, it will never happen.

For example, you can leverage what you're willing to do.

"I am going to make $500 a month and my goal is to achieve this in the next six months. I'm going to do whatever it takes because I want to be able to take my kids to Disneyland every single year, even though I only have seven hours a week to devote."

If your company is product-based, there may be scientists, experts, studies or other company leaders who have documented success that you can leverage.

7. Be Brief: The Preview to the Movie

There's power in brevity. If you give someone too much information, it'll only bog them down and prevent them from saying yes or no to looking at your business opportunity. You want to give them just enough information to pique their interest—the preview to the movie. Only then should you use your tools.

8. Ask for Help

If you're getting stuck anywhere in your business, ask for help. Reach out to people on your team. It could be your upline, sideline or downline. You can reach out via Zoom, phone or group chat.

9. Third Party Tools

Leverage tools to grow your business. It could be Facebook groups, a catchy video, a webinar using Zoom, etc.

10. Authenticity

It's really tough to be you when you're trying to be someone else. When I tried to be exactly like my $30 million mentor, I sucked. When I learned to take the success principles I learned from him and apply them to my personality, that's when I crushed it. I became the number one recruiter out of nine insurers. I learned to extract the principles and be the bold version of me.

11. Solve a Problem

When you're recruiting, you're solving a problem. People don't buy what they need. They buy what they want. They buy a solution to a problem that they have. Every decision made is based on emotion. Even logical decisions are based on emotion to create the logic.

12. Show Them That They Can Do it Too

Whether it's a lead, a new recruit or a longtime team member, people will still ask themselves, "can I do it?". Your job is to show them that they can by leading by example.

BLITZ WEEK

In network marketing, a week of all out, pedal to the metal recruiting is called a blitz week. Why is a huge week of recruiting so valuable? Because it amplifies your efforts and gives you confidence. It generates frenetic energy and generates momentum. When you learn to crush your blitz week, you create a skill that can be used again, as well as taught to your team for exponential growth.

Execute one blitz week twice a year. I promise you'll see results if you do this.

You Blitz Week Blueprint

1. Clear your schedule for the whole week. You don't want to get sidetracked while you're laser-focused on recruiting - it will kill your inertia.

2. Decide beforehand who you're looking to recruit and be **as specific as you can** about the avatar you create for them.

   For example, I might look for females who are 30 to 40 years old, who are active but need a little extra energy.

   Other examples:

   - business builders working in real estate because they have great communication skills.

   - elementary school teachers who want to supplement their income

3. **Contact 50:** Schedule time to contact 50 people and reach out to them. It can be via text, voice messaging, email or phone call. Invite them to your launch call.

4. **Launch Call With Your Upline:** Your upline can help you leverage your credibility. Find someone who is more experienced than you to help with launch calls during Blitz Week. A lot of times it will be your sponsor who guides you through it, but it doesn't have to be.

   Your launch call can be held via Zoom, a live video in a Facebook group or in person. Remember to fully embrace the bold version of you and let your genuine passion for helping people shine through when you speak.

5. **Take your struggle and turn it into your story.** During your launch call, people will want to know your story before they begin to trust you. What's something you can share that's vulnerable? Maybe you were sick and tired of not having the extra income, extra time, not being able to travel or just playing it too small.

   Then, share what you're excited about for the future of your life and how the company is an integral part of it. Make it short and powerful.

ONE-DAY SPRINT

Once a month, schedule a single day to do a condensed version of blitz actions, which I call a One-Day Sprint. Combined with your two blitz weeks per year, this is killer for accelerating your business growth. Again, you may not see the results right away, but one day in the future you will reap the rewards for your hard work.

DAILY METHOD OF OPERATION (DMO)

Your Daily Method of Operation is your blueprint for accelerating growth. This is an example of one that I created for a company. It's called 1-5-1-5-1. Feel free to use it, modify it or make up your own DMO. However you do your DMO, it must consist of income producing activities that you can complete every day.

1 New Social Media Post

Your social media post could be live video or a regular post, whatever you're most comfortable with. Only two days a week should be about business. The other five days are non-business related for exposure, for people to get to know and like you.

5 Reach-Outs (non-business related)

Reaching out is part of the game of networking, and proper networking is one of the secrets to building your network marketing business. It's so essential that I wrote a book on it—you can find it at **www.thegameofnetworking.com**.

I have been reaching out to 300 people a month for over 13 years and it's all non-business related. Like we went over earlier, I don't do fake chitchat. I find something we have in common and make a human connection with my lead. I leave them a voice message and it's usually 20 seconds or less.

5 reach-outs a day doesn't take that long, but can you imagine if you did 10 a day? You can adjust these numbers to be higher or lower depending on your skillset, personal sales style and how much effort you want to put in.

1 New Ask

Every day, you've got to **ask one person** to look at your product/ service/business opportunity. Reach-outs and posts prime your leads for the ask (so it won't be a random hard sell out of nowhere), but if you don't ever get around to asking, guess what? You won't recruit, you won't grow, you won't help anyone, and you won't make any money.

Your number of asks will obviously be much higher during One-Day Sprints or Blitz Week.

5 New Friends

This one relates back to Tier One, #3. Add 5 new friends on social media every day. This is an easy way to add to your lead list, which you are responsible for growing. If you find yourself running out of leads too quickly, then you can add more than 5 per day.

1 Follow-Up

Follow up with people you've previously invited to look at the business or product/service. These people haven't said yes or no yet, and have agreed to let you keep them updated on your progress; you need to follow up periodically until you get a yes or no. This could be in the form of a third-party validation or a normal one-on-one follow-up.

With my 1-5-1-5-1 method (again, this is only one example of a DMO) you're focusing on Tier One and making that your daily priority. You're creating exposure with posts. You're never running out of leads because you're adding new friends, keeping in touch with them, and you're asking.

TRACK EVERYTHING

Once you've figured out what your DMO is, track the activities in a spreadsheet that you can share with your accountability partner. It keeps you accountable, and it serves as a useful tool to evaluate your progress, and refine your approach based on what's working and what's not working.

My goal with this eBook was to provide value for you so that you can take your business to the next level, no matter how new or seasoned you are in this business. I had incredible mentors who helped me, and I love that I'm able to pass it on to help you. I want to see you win! I hope you found massive value. More importantly, I hope you take these tips and implement some into your business.

Thanks for reading, I appreciate you.

If you haven't already go invest in **www.thegameofconquering.com** and take your business to the next level!

CPSIA information can be obtained
at www.ICGtesting.com
Printed in the USA
LVHW080716160920
666055LV00007BA/911